The

Soul Within

The Journey of the Soul Within

Poetry of Healing and Transformation

Gillian Small

LEON SMITH

PUBLISHING

www.leonsmithpublishing.com

I dedicate this book to those who have ever felt hopeless, defeated, and stuck in life. I let them know they are loved, they are worthy, and they are magnificent souls who are still remembering who they really are.

Praise for *The Journey of the Soul Within:*

"Gillian's book, *The Journey of the Soul Within: Poetry of Healing and Transformation,* is a wonderfully poetic, healing, and inspirational contribution to anyone who reads it. I love how Gillian can contribute to other people's growth and transformation by writing and channelling these stories after completing her own inner work. I also love that her intention is to inspire, motivate, and support others who are also travelling on their own journey of transformation and growth. Her message throughout is that your inward journey is where you reclaim what is already yours—your wisdom, empowerment, self-worth, and magnificence. Reading these pages will inspire you to go out and use the techniques she has and be the best version of yourself. Enjoy what you read and reach into your power and wisdom. You are dearly loved."

> Jenny Johnston, Founder of Quantum EFT for the Soul, EFT Universe Trainer, and Bestselling Author of *Tapping into Past Lives* and *Your Past Life Inheritance,* www.quantumeft.com.au

"True transformation begins with the recognition that we hold beliefs that have been bestowed upon us from the world we live in. Gillian's poetry masterfully reveals the cosmic power within that can shatter old beliefs, and allow us to stand fully and wholly within that power. Her words and energy vibrate from each page, lighting the way to what is yours to claim."

> Corby Furrow, founder Radiant Core Solutions, EFT Practitioner, and Bestselling Author of *What's Self-Love Got to Do With It?*

"*The Journey of the Soul Within* is a rare treasure of a book. Author Gillian Small vulnerably shares her healing journey in lyrically poignant phrases that inspire her reader to more powerfully embrace their own difficult times. This gift of transformational poetry from a true spiritual companion is one to truly savour. Every page eloquently encourages us to tap into the truth of our inherent worthiness and brilliance."

> Nancy Forrester, Founder and Executive Director, National Emotional Freedom Techniques Training Institute, NeftTI.com

"Reality shifts when self-awareness enters and allows us to start to take control of our thoughts, feelings, and way of being in the world. Becoming self-aware opens the door to lasting change and empowers us to make the most nourishing choices in every moment. *The Journey of the Soul Within* is a beautiful book of poetry to help inspire you along your path of self-awareness, inner growth, and healing."

Judy Howsam, **Reiki Master, Teacher, Practitioner, Certified Emotional Success Coach (NeftTI)**, and an **Accredited Certified EFT Practitioner**, www.judysreiki.com

Contents

REBIRTH

LIBERATION

Acknowledgments

I am so grateful and blessed for my family, friends, mentors, and colleagues who have supported and encouraged me and who had faith in my writings, at a time when I didn't. These people saw the inspiration, passion, and love in my stories and poems before I did!

Initially when I was told: *You should compile your writings into a book of short stories,* I thought people were just being nice and trying to make me feel good. However, over time with continued feedback and beautiful comments from them— and a little bit of Emotional Freedom Techniques (EFT) on my end to release the block that *no one would be interested*—I finally felt the calling to create this book.

I am ever so grateful for several people in my life who believed my writings were worthy, but most importantly, I had to feel and know they were worthy before proceeding. Everything comes from within, including validation, acknowledgment, and acceptance.

I thank Jenny Johnston, my Quantum EFT for the Soul Instructor, who was the first person to suggest that I compile my writings into a book. I thank Nancy Forrester, Theresa Marchotte, Judy Howsam, Laurie Booker, Corby Furrow, Lisa Bosworth, Salima Bhanwadia, Lori Nott-Salter, Linda Chalmers, Elaine Leufkens, Brenda Lee Osmond, Denise McFarlane, Shea Small, Aidan Small, and Liam Small.

I thank the catalysts in my life who upset and triggered me, which led me to my own inner journey work, to heal those upsets and emotional wounds, and ultimately to find my voice, power, courage, and self-love.

I thank the Universe who unwaveringly and unconditionally supports, guides, heals, and loves me.

Introduction

This book is a compilation of short stories and poetry. I usually write my stories after I have completed some inner work to clear, let go, and release something—whether it be upsetting emotions, circumstances, or a trigger or realization that was not serving my best interests or that was robbing my peace of mind and joy. After doing my work to release what is not serving me, I feel more peaceful, compassionate, loving, and empowered and then feel an energy of inspiration to write about my journey in the form of a short story or poem.

My writings are often channeled from my higher self, my guides, or Spirit. My writings are a result of my own healing and transformations through self-growth work. I write to help guide, support, motivate, and inspire others along their path in life.

If you are in a place where you feel stuck, hard-done-by, cheated, unmotivated, grieving, resentful, hopeless, or being too hard on yourself and others, I hope that my writings will inspire you to do some inner soul work to help release any emotional baggage or unhealed, unresolved karmic debris. Inner soul work allows more space for peace, joy, and purpose into your life.

We are all Energy and all One in this vast cosmic Universe. Even though my writings reflect my own pain and suffering, healing, and transformation, I would like you to know that if I can heal from past trauma and upsets, you can too!

Keep this book on your nightstand and read one or two stories each night before going to bed. Allow the messages of self-worth, self-love, and self-acceptance inspire you to reach deep within your soul and receive that *knowing and remembering* that we are all innately born with.

Hear these messages: *I am worthy. I am lovable. I am magnificent.*

After reading and placing the book back down, place your hand on your heart and repeat this affirmation:

Tonight, only good things.
Tonight, only good things.
Tonight, only good things.
Tomorrow, only good things.

Then take a deep breath, breathing in peace, and a long exhale, breathing out compassion. Allow the beautiful message meant for you to be absorbed while you sleep. Let the ether of the Universe wrap you in its arms and bask your soul in loving light. May you have the most beautiful dreams and awaken in the energy of love and light.

We are all born in the light of worthiness and joy, and often life, people, and judgments rob of us who we really are. I am here to let you know that as a being of divine love and light: *You are worthy, You are magnificent, You are love!*

All you ever need is already within you, so stop seeking it from others and your external world. Instead, travel inwards and reclaim all that is already yours.

Empowerment

Empowerment: *The emotion one feels when finally stepping into authenticity, speaking truth unwaveringly, and standing one's ground—with confidence and pride*

Goddess of Light

She's a Goddess of light,
an angelic soul, soft, but holds a good fight.

Energy between Light and Dark.
It's stronger, making its mark.

This dimension only holds space for the bright,
no room for the Dark to manifest its ugly fight.

She sees, she knows, she's a powerful soul—
wise and strong, no room for another to uphold.

The Dark tries with all its sorry might
to chip away at her beautiful frequency, with such sad fight.

Lo and behold, there's no room for Dark to pull her down.
She's made of light, surrounded by angels, guides, psychics,
    healers— a light the Dark cannot get around.

Dark used to be powerful in old energy, it's true,
but it's no longer welcome in fifth dimension: no room for
    you.

Try as it may to continue the same old ways
of spells and dark thoughts directed Light's way.
But this foolish nonsense of ways will drown Dark, deep in
    decay.

The energy between Light and Dark, so it goes.
only making Light stronger that nothing else can uphold.

Try as Dark likes to continue the fight,
but Light will always see through and win each day and
    night.

For Light reigns power over all the that's directed her way.
She's so light and so bright that she wishes the Dark well
    and prays for Divine to help it along its way.

The powerful Goddess shoots her divine arrows of light
right at the Dark blasting away its nasty fight.

The Universe reigns the Goddess so true,
applauding her strength and energy, whilst no dark can
    seep through.

While the Dark sadly continued this energetic fight,
the Goddess retaliated with pure divine light.

She Spread Her Wings

She spawned her wings of golden light,
    cascading through waves of time and plight.
Iridescent shimmers breaking free,
    from lifetimes of dependent patriarchy.
Her body swayed, connecting with divine femininity,
    releasing beliefs of how things are supposed to be.

Sparkles of radiant universal dust illuminated her soul with
    such brilliant gust.

Breathing and sensing to the sounds of her own soul,
    as her wings opened and fluttered, transmuting old to
    gold.
It was time to set her spirit free,
    spreading her wings for humanity.

Time to Fly

She could hear the waves moving closer and closer,
carrying the echoes of their past voices.
Her past voices, the incessant noises.

They rose and crashed. Waves thrashing
against Earth's bountiful rocky cliff side. Crashing
against her beliefs that no longer served.
Smashing them into the ground, no longer to be found.

The waves ripped and tore
through the templates of the past.
They could no longer rehash
that which was ready to be cast.

Her feathered wings, ripe
they had always been, yet smothered in unwanted screams.
Now done with the programming that wished
her no good, the waves teased her to spread
those wings, as she so could.

Fluttering open with divine wisdom,
her wings deflected the waves prism.
"How will you ever know if you can fly,
    if you never use your wings?"

And with an inner knowing
and a gleeful sigh
she soared, she flew
way up high.

Karma

For the creepers that like to creep
and the peepers who like to make others weep,
don't forget karma sees what you reap.

Once you block
yet continue to stalk,
you're the only one creating a mock.

Maybe you're bored
and nothing better to do,
try minding your own business. Or haven't you a clue?

For all that you are
and all that you do,
the heavens above still see you.

Casting waves of deceit,
playing those for some fools
unless they retreat.

This is your time.
This is your life.
How do you wish to create it just right?

Make your intentions and actions pure from the heart,
lest karma see fit how your soul shall depart.

The creepers can change for better or worse,
and so goes their game, often with curse.

The Universe sees,
and energy knows,
what you put out always unfolds.

Karma's a beautiful thing.
It's real, just listen to it sing.
Its brilliant chants will boomerang back with zing.

We Are Creators

I connect my feet to Mother Earth,
grounding in her grassy hearth.

Nature's sensations embrace my stance,
flowing vibrations like the perfect dance.

The sun pours down on my naked skin,
opening my arms to all within.

The glorious skies in all their mist
blazing energies from Gaia's bliss.

And as the gates appear so far,
they shine on me like long-lost stars.

I return to the essence of who I am—
wisdom and truth, as I rewrite my own program.

I am my God.
I am my Creator.
I am my Temple,
as all are inside me.
This is divine truth and so it shall be.

Self-Love and Acceptance

Self-Love and Acceptance: *A deep-rooted regard for one's own self-care and self-respect for mind, body, and soul*

The Connection Within

Roaming and buzzing and all alone,
searching throughout the great unknown.

Disconnected and scared.

Where was her place?
Was it all a disgrace?

Foundations created by beliefs of separation.
Generations that forced a cruel dilation.

Surrounded by many, yet alone in her world.
No justification for her life unhurled.

All that had been taught through the minds of her tribe,
Prejudiced conglomerates unseen dissected her pride.

Piece by piece, the learnings she was taught
no longer had relevance in this life that she sought.

And just when her purpose and meaning was about to
    come crumbling down,
in came her twin, her spirit, her soul-part was found.

For it's not what you think, not another *one* per say.
Yet she connected with source, her inner divine that day.

He came flying in to support her and connect on a level so
   deep.
He was her other half and so eager to take the big leap.

She accepted and reconnected, to herself, the divine
   masculine feminine reunited at last—
a reunion of ancient alchemy from her long-lost past.

*And so, her search of seeking and fulfillment from external ones
   came to a halt.*

For all that she needed was already within,
resurrecting and pollinating with her very own twin.

No need to look outside of oneself for happiness, peace,
   love, joy, protection.
The company we seek is inside on a divine connection.

Blessings for all those who are so vulnerable and open.
Thus, they shall reap the benefits of love unspoken.

This is our time, dear ones, to take that journey within.
For it is in this sacred space where true love begins.

The Girl Who Finally Found the Love She Was Looking For

She was a lost little soul,
not able to follow the mold.
Watching her friends laugh and in love
while she sat at home like an injured dove.

She thought no one cares,
who would even dare?
She was a sweet sixteen
with no boy on the scene.

Feeling unloved and misunderstood,
only wanting what her outside world was not willing to
    give.

Bringing these fables and myths
about how love should exist
into her older years
only deepened her fears.

What was this Valentine's Day really about?
For it only made her want to pout.

Year after year, it became quite clear,
No boy or man could match her sphere.
Her perception of love was one not real.
It was based on illusion, myth, fairy tales—not ideal.

It was not until her journey inwards, and faith came from
    above,
did she meet with her one true love.
A love that can only be found from within,
could illuminate her soul, her spark, and make her heart
    spin.

As she began to emanate through her own self-worth,
her lack of self-validation, love, and appreciation began a
    rebirth.

And so, this once-lost little girl hugged her heart and soul
    so tight,
her shadows, her flaws, and her brilliant essence of light.
Learning to love herself from the sacred depths within,
emanating this brilliance to the world and all akin.

Mother's Day

Her desire to birth of selfless love,
to create and embrace her divine unique space.
Offering herself in all her ways,
her grace and flow embrace his pace.

Together they love, honour, and procreate,
Surrendering and allowing for what takes place.
The seeds of love blossom and grow,
flourishing in her womb from the depths of her soul.

She laughs and cries tears of fear and joy
as she births her beautiful little boys.
A promise of devotion and love so pure,
it spills through the Universe to her heart so clear.

An undying love birthed right from the start,
to practice patience and compassion to her babes—
    unconditional love from the heart.
Her grace and honour to be their goddess of light,
a mom to love them and hold a space for their flight.

Mothering in the best ways she knows how,
to raise and praise their moments and days.
No one said it would be easy: you can't learn from a book.
Blessed motherhood—it's unconditional love without a
    hook.

She holds the space for her boys to grow
in ways they continue to surprise and show.
Till the day she passes to the other side,
her undying love for her boys will suffice.

Motherhood taught her patience,
compassion, and unconditional love.
Full of deep gratitude for this beautiful
and divine experience from above.

It Was Her Time

The beautiful mermaid swam and splashed in the cold, dark ocean waters. Her feminine human top half and feminine fish-like bottom half gently pushed her through the currents beneath the surface. She was a divine elemental. She couldn't be happier. She was overcome with joy and freedom, allowing herself to swim and flow with the currents of life. Splishing and splashing away. Even though it didn't quite feel like home, she was certainly free to be her true authentic, divinely beautiful, and powerful mermaid self.

When the fun for her was complete, she swiftly and elegantly swam to the surface. Her head perched where air and water meet. She gazed towards the radiant moonlit surface of the ocean waters, peering towards the horizon. The moon shone brightly, as its divine luminescent light was showing her the way. She could hear and feel the other mermaids around her, feeding her with support and encouragement.

Delving once again into the depths of the cold ocean waters, she chose to swim in the direction of the iridescent moonlight. Still not knowing exactly where the divinity of this light would take her, she knew she was headed in the most divine direction. This time she trusted herself. The mermaid knew it was her time. Time to follow the truth of what was in her heart and soul.

The Name of the Game

Twin Flame was the name of the game.
No one was to blame, no one to shame.

In the crowded room, the electricity went zoom.
One could hear it, see it, feel it as it soared and boomed.

Enough about the twin flame. It's just a game.
Comprised of illusion, an over-romanticized conclusion.

Grandiose ideas, sugarcoating hearts.
Placating with their mind, their soul, and their smarts.

Catalysts at best, putting life to the test.
Is their goal peace and joy? Or to rock the boat? One might
    implore.

Energy connecting, flames resurrecting—at the cost of
    hearts dissecting.
The flames beneath their feet that led them to meet.

The intoxicating chaos
was all but a drain,
but not a loss.

For the name of the game in this mysterious notion, we call
    Twin Flame,
is to come together, yet part again.

Each on their way, learning lessons of today.
Going within is the only way to win.

As one might see,
just let them be.

Two, each on their own,
and divinely guided towards the light.
They will be shown.

Healing

Healing*: The challenging, yet rewarding process of becoming aware of, acknowledging, and recovering from past hurts, upsets, and illnesses to becoming healthy, peaceful, and joyful once again*

Letter to My Younger Self

Dear Gillian,

When your parents fight, it's not about you. They are loving you in the best way they know how. They don't know any better, even though they are adults and you think they should know better. (You are correct.) But they don't know, and they are doing the best they can on the limited knowledge they have—and none of it has anything to do with you.

They probably go to bed feeling guilty most nights, wondering what you're thinking because they don't know how to be vulnerable or authentic or how to communicate with you.

I hear what you're thinking: *But they're the adults*.

Bless you, Little One. They weren't taught how to communicate with an open heart, so how are they to do that with you? I hope one day you'll understand. Most importantly, I want you to know it has nothing to do with you.

I also need to let you know that all those times you were left on your own—scared, lonely, and sad with no one to confide in or laugh with—again, it had nothing to do with you. Your parents were overwhelmed and preoccupied with disagreeing amongst themselves about finances and Lord knows what else. I assure you it had nothing to do with you.

All those times they rolled their eyes at you or scoffed when you laughed or shrieked out. You were expressing sheer delight at the silliest thing, or the wonders of the world, and you decided: *What's the point in being happy? No one gives a damn anyways.*

Let me tell you: *Go ahead, Little One, and laugh to your heart's content!*

Don't let their miserable outlook on life take away from your joy, happiness, and love. Their distrust of your happiness has nothing to do with you. It's their story, their history, their lack of emotional freedom, and their fear that joy could be swiftly taken away from them. It has nothing to do with you.

That time when you were a little bit older and thought no one cared and wouldn't even notice if you were missing? That time when you swallowed the bottle of painkillers hoping it would all go away? Let me tell you why it didn't work. Your angels and the Universe knew you had a purpose. For all the emotional pain and suffering you were feeling, they knew you had the strength to pull through because you were needed here on this planet of ours.

You are needed to show those suffering that there is hope, there is love, there is meaning, and there is purpose. You are an inspiration of hope and a beacon of light to show others that they too are worthy of their place on this planet.

So, I'm here to tell you to relax and enjoy life and all that it has to offer. You are divinely guided. You are divinely protected. You are divinely supported. You are divinely loved.

The Universe has your back, Little One.

Letting Go

Their gnarled claws dug in so tight,
rapturous teeth biting in sheer delight.
The torturous momentum of back and forth
pulled at their souls without much fight.
Back and forth and back and forth they went,
knowing full well it wasn't quite right.

Time and time again the struggle was real,
although the illusion was not ready to reveal.
Their hearts opened and closed with the dark and the light,
as the vulnerabilities and stubbornness tore open with
    might.

The contracts that said: *You must do this to heal,*
to love unconditionally, it does reveal.
Despite the lessons, all was clear.
It was not meant to be in this realm, my dear.

They pulled back their claws and softened the bite,
the back and forth and stubbornness, gave up the big fight.
Releasing the karmic debris, between she and he,
they surrendered to not meant to be.

Thanking one another for their roles in this part,
they released their grip and slowly, yet lovingly, drifted
    apart.

Divine Mercy Day

And once she remembered the sacred divinity
and soul-truths of the magnificence of who she really was,
she never had to look outside again.
All that she ever needs, exists within.

Someone told me last Sunday was Divine Mercy Sunday—
that God forgives our sins, always, but that day God had
mercy on us. Or something to that extent.

As I am more spiritual (that which comes from within) than
religious (that which is external), I responded, "To me, every
day is divine mercy day, as I can choose to forgive and have
mercy on myself and others any day, anytime I choose to."
We are all free to choose: choose what we eat, choose what
to wear, choose the people we associate with, choose our
methods of learning, and choose what to believe deep within
our soul.

Some choose to look at God as a sign of faith and healing,
and others choose to go within. Some choose both! Some
even consider Source or Universe as another form of *God*.
Heck, even a favourite tree or rock could be God to someone.
It's called *free choice,* and it's an empowering and beautiful
thing.

What I choose to believe is that We are God/Source/
Creative Source/Universe—call it what you may—as we are

made from the stars, cells, atoms, molecules, unconditional love, and healing light.

God exists within each of us.
– Kryon, Source entity

My own pain and suffering led me to a path of healing, forgiveness, and compassion. Within that challenging, sacred, and beautiful journey called *personal growth,* I rediscovered spirituality.

And on this journey, I found the more I looked externally for healing and happiness, the more frustrated I became. It is only when I discovered methods that invited me to go inwards that I started to heal. Some modalities that helped me to go inwards safely were yoga, Reiki, Emotional Freedom Techniques (EFT), and Quantum EFT. There are a variety of methods to assist one to go inwards; these are my favourites.

These are amazing tools that we can use when we feel the need to. We can go inwards to shift anger to forgiveness, hatred to compassion, and dark to light. Therefore, I believe we don't need a special place to go or person or guru or something external to feel forgiveness or mercy for ourselves or others. We can do that ourselves, as all that we ever need is already given to us and is already within us. We don't need to wait for a certain day or for anyone to have mercy on us, for that comes from within and can be done any day.

This is my own spiritually aligned belief regarding forgiveness and compassion that has rebirthed within me profound healing, joy, happiness, gratitude, and peace. Others are more than welcome to their beliefs and opinions that hopefully bring them a life of peace, joy, and happiness. That is all I'd ever want for my friends and family on this sacred planet Earth that is our home.

The Storm or the Present Moment?

It was calm and peaceful. The sun shone. The grass grew. The rain wept. Thunder roared. But, it was the way it was supposed to be. All was well. It was calm. It was peaceful.

Then lightning stepped in. It seared with its lightning bolt. Its energy ignited. It pierced. It said *yes!* It said *no!* Confusion? Passion? It was not rational. Was it? What was it?

Illusion? Reality? What is illusion? What is reality? It's all ruthless really. It's all love really. What is it all really, anyways?

All we have is time after time. Year after year. Life after life. Soul after soul. He said. She said. Whom are you going to believe? What do you choose to believe? What does your programming say; what does it want you to believe? Is it serving you now?

Does it all really matter? All we have is *now* anyways. How can the sun be present if it's thinking about the clouds? How can the rain be present if it's worried about the sun? How can thunder be so loud if it's concerned about the strike of lightning? Is Gaia stressed about the flow? No.

Then human need not be either. Flow. Soar. Allow. Surrender. Release. Live. Love. It's a mixed bag. Is it? Which one of the above comes first? you ask. What is the sequence? I don't know. Do you? Does anyone? Is there a sequence?

All I know is that as tough and as challenging as it may be, paradoxically, this is where one is asked to be in the present moment.

Does the sun get angry when the clouds move in? No. Does the grass cry when the rain pours its heavy tears? No. Does thunder get scared when lightning is more threatening? No.

Each has its own job. Its own responsibility. Its own love. Each moves, syncs, aligns, flows, allows, grows, and surrenders to one another. Humans can too. Can we? One day? What about today?

Letting Go of Past Lives

I could have ended it long before
that time when you choose to shut the door.

The isolation left in my face
was not more miserable than you in my space.

Countless times I begged to leave,
but often succumbed to your very plea.

Was just one more added to your lengthy list
of those whose energies could not resist.

Fruitless times of ups and downs,
spinning my head 'round and 'round.

My clouded judgment cloaked in fears,
choking back the endless tears.

A ticking time bomb one might say,
the bomb that left us in disarray.

Until I saw it for what it really was,
a disillusionment with no good cause.

One was pure and one was not.
And so, inside the light I sought.

The light that shone so very bright,
that scared away the dark knight.

Peace, joy, freedom at last.
Good riddance to the heavy past.

Last Goodbyes

She looked upon him with wondering eyes,
    dismissing the blatant manipulation and lies.

Her heart so full and divinely pure
    bought into the words no spell could cure.

A magician is light and blessed in soul,
    while the trickster's dark ways cast shadows untold.

Her spirit of light caught his dark eyes,
    and he clung to her in superficial disguise.

Ashamed to reveal the truth he so hid,
    afraid she could see his façade that forbid.

Until one day, the maiden of light
    broke through the chains of chaos and plight.

Casting away his deceptive spells,
    she untangled herself from a disillusioned hell.

With a farewell full of self-worth and high vibes,
    she gracefully said her last goodbyes.

Rebirth

Rebirth: *The spiritual process whereby one heals enough to recover from past trauma and upsets to live life differently, often from a more positive, purposeful, and compassionate manner*

Rebirth of Herself

From a young age, she felt so much despair,
but could not find the right way for herself to repair.

She searched high and low,
above and below.

Looked in the gardens, under the rocks, to the trees,
but could not find ease.

Reading this book and that book,
but could not find the hook.

She met that teacher and that preacher,
and looked for a guru that she could look up to.

Searching for answers on how to be
peaceful and live happily.

Then one day, she shed her cocoon,
leaving behind her outdated costume.

Realizing no one could save her, she looked within,
beyond the depths of her pale freckled skin.

She decided she had the power, the light and the will,
and began her own process to morph with such skill.

Like a caterpillar who morphs to a butterfly,
she too began her rebirth from crawling to soaring high.

The Mermaid

she swam the oceans
deep and wide
longing, yearning, desiring
something more inside

lonely and empty
with nowhere to go
unsure of her destination
still untold

her blue-scaled tail
pushed her along the way
while her gold-laden fin
directed her course that day

looking here
and looking there
to the mountains, the trees
and the iridescent air

yet it was only in the unknown
waters of depths so deep
did she find solace
and peace to redeem her keep

transmuting the dark and pain
of resentment and shame

alchemizing the shadows
to love and light again

after navigating through waters so deep
and riding the waves so steep
did she finally emerge
into her own and ready to leap

swimming away
from the dark and decay
finding peace in her new
rebirth that day

Phoenix Rising

Shattered and scathed,
her soul plummeted to the ground.
Crumbling and demoralizing,
Earth's haven struck her down.

The pains of renunciation
drove her heart beyond what it was worth.
scathing and anticipating
the worst from this hearth.

Plagued by invisible
demons and energetic sparks,
the karmic debris no longer
permitted to make its mark.

Lashing and thrashing
this energy to its end.
Seeing every last molecule dissipate,
making no amend.

Battered and shattered
as the stake shears through her soul.
In the distance, the smug laughter
gleefully unfolds.

The atrocities of retribution
so stern on his face,

she no longer wavered
in his disgraceful space.

Vile, a villain
where only ego saved face,
wanting to dominate his prey,
control and manipulate from a demoralizing place.

Shattered and crumbled
and scathed to her soul,
she cleared the last remnants
from this smouldering hole.

Rising up like a Phoenix
from ashes burning the ground,
blasting old energy
that once kept her bound.

Rising and shining,
so glad to be rid.
Empowered in light,
she shone through the grid.

Flames illuminated
as she brilliantly rose,
casting pillars of light
through old shadows now closed.

Aware and awakened,
enlightened and brightened,

wiser and free
of past energetic debris.

Wings set free
and spreading so wide,
rising, illuminating light,
so radiant and glorified.

Sun-Kissed Bliss

Sun-kissed with radiant bliss.
You can no longer touch the essence of this.

My courage and strength to go within.
To clear and release that which does not bring peace.

Balance is key in cleaning up the debris.
Letting go of what and who does not serve me.

Standing tall like the tree.
Being grounded is key.

Swaying my branches to winds of the past.
Shedding layers that are not meant to last.

Standing tall and proud, feet anchored, and head held high.
Swimming in divine energies radiating in star drops from
    the sky.

.

The Youniverse Within

I look up at the sky, and what I see
Is the cosmos of you, the Universe in me.

The clouds and the stars beckon us to see
our heritage, journey, and how we came to be.

Magnificent and brilliant, we make up the One.
In all that we are, connected, not undone.

We will always share a love so divine.
Gaia our Mother Earth—messages and synchronicities—is
    our sign.

Holding us near and dear,
Our beloved ancestors, their channelings clear.

If you pay attention, you will believe.
You won't question your divinity; you will receive.

Look and gaze up at the wonders all around.
The same wonders are in you, it is found.

For all that we are and all we will be,
The divinity of One, birthed in You and in Me.

Liberation

Liberation*: The act of thriving and experiencing freedom that characterizes life after the process of healing, self-growth, and inner journey soul work*

Exhilaration at Its Finest

The rubber hit the concrete.
She heard the pounding of the ground.
A jolt of climactic energy bolted up from the bottom,
connecting with her crown.

Pulsating blood cells expanding,
shooting up like a light,
the blood rushing through her veins,
circulating in unwavering delight.

The repetitive actions of up and down,
increased her energies all around.
Feeling coolness enter her throat
was magical and profound.

Her body exhilarating
in the energy and the rush,
heartbeats and adrenaline racing,
causing her cheeks to colour a pink flush.

Alas the thrill was over,
and this blissful time was up,
drinking in the air
from God's universal cup.

She was healthy and flourishing,
feeling complete and whole—
relishing in new vibrations,
her mind, body, and soul.

The Magician

You are the magician.
Go within and listen.
What does your heart say?
What do your thoughts portray?

Let go of blaming, for you have the key.
To make peace with your past and let your magic set you
    free.

The future you hold
is still untold.
Let your magic ignite
all your desires in sight.

It's quite simple you see.
Nothing external can jeopardize thee.

For you hold the power, the magic, my dear.
To create a life that is simple and clear.

You are the awakened one of divinity bright.
Let go of others that hold back your flight.

Let them go, dear ones, with grace and love.
You will reap rewards most only dream of.

Believe from the depth of your soul.
You hold the key to make your magic unfold.

It's within You. Believe! Believe!
For this is where your answer lies.
　　Trust me.

The Staircase of Life

In the staircase of life, there can be much strife,
    but there's solace in knowing life is about flowing.

What mindset you choose can give highs or blues.
    Tap away all that does not serve, making room for
    energy that you deserve.

Make sure that your walk matches the vibration of your
    talk.
    The Universe sees and the Universe knows all that your
    thoughts and intentions unfold.

So with a clean slate, strike the mark you choose to make.
    Are your intentions clear and pure? Do they reflect light
    that reassures?

Be as you might and be as you will. Perhaps one day the
    stairs you walk will take you uphill.

The Dark Knight Who Chiseled Hearts and the Radiant Maiden Who Rose Above It All

His shining armor and suave choice of words portrayed him to be the most sought-after knight in the countryside. The maidens fell at his beckoning call. However, the trail of broken hearts he left behind began a vicious cycle within his broken soul. The coiled snake that wound tightly around his aching heart would grow to bind tighter and tighter as he searched the countryside for his other half. The coiled snake protected his childhood broken heart and grew within him, each and every search a disappointment.

He carried with him the most glamorous, illuminous golden sword that also encapsulated the pure but naive hearts of the beautiful maidens. Upon every meeting with each maiden, his sword deeply chiseled, stealing yet another beam of light from their hearts and souls. This left the pure maidens devastated and betrayed, yet boosted the knight's soul and sadly, his ego. For he searched, used, stole, and chiseled the maidens' hearts, souls, and ultimately their light to fulfill his own lack esteem, confidence, and self-worth.

After a long overdue rest from searching the countryside for the purest of light, the knight came unto his own. Seeking isolation and retreat from his search and himself, he took to solitude. As synchronicity should have her way, the Universe felt the timing right. During his reclusion, and without any effort of search from the knight's soul, he found his other half. The one with the brightest and purest of light. Although he was caught off guard, he was magically encapsulated by this beautiful maiden, as he knew right away, she was the one he had been searching for all those years.

Yet sadly within his time of isolation and seclusion, he chose to blame the people and world around him for his loneliness and pain, instead of looking within to heal the broken childhood trauma that scarred his heart and soul. And thus, the coiled snake that lay repressed around his broken heart and still protected him, remained.

The dashing knight professed and declared his love for his one and only fairest and purest of maidens. However, the more he fell in love with her, the tighter the snake coiled around his heart. Without delving into the lessons and learnings and healing from his past, there was no moving forward in love. And, as history would have it, out came the illuminous, brilliant sword and—possibly unbeknownst to the knight himself—the sword began to chisel away at his fair maiden's heart and soul.

So, the sharp point of his sword pierced through this most beautiful and brightest of all the maidens in the countryside. As he so selfishly chiseled and stole her light, she began to collapse into the darkness of him. The coiled snake was scary and so tight, there was nothing either one of them could do. Suddenly, the fair maiden heard the screams and pleas of all the other maidens in the countryside who had fallen prey and decayed at the whims of the dark knight. She dove within the depths of her heart and soul and harnessed her source power.

Her radiance and divinity shone brighter than ever before. With her purest intentions, she magically aligned her own heart through the ethers with all those who had walked, loved, cried, decayed, and collapsed before her in the name of love. With this, she rose from the depths of defeat and brokenness, grasped the handle of the sword with her hands, and ever so powerfully stood her ground. With divine love and light, she pulled the piercing end of the sword gracefully out of her heart. The blood that gushed from her soul as the sword left her body flowed down the physicality of her and transformed miraculously and brilliantly to the most vibrant pink and yellow flowers never seen before, even in the most magnificent gardens surrounding the countryside.

With gust and valour, she quickly and generously spread this radiant and divinely purest light back to all the fair maidens whose light had been stained and drained from them in their hopes of everlasting love with the dark knight. Their beautiful love and light had been replenished with overflowing divine source energy, and they became whole and complete within their own beautiful divinity. They no longer needed or succumbed to the whims, charm, or disillusionment of fantastical fairy tales. They no longer needed to wait for their one and only. All they ever needed was already within them.

There was such an abundance of light emanating from these synchronistically aligned events, that the dark knight's purest maiden sent him as much light as his own heart and soul required so that he no longer felt compelled to search externally, recklessly breaking hearts along his way. She only hoped one day he too would find the courage and strength to go within his own soul to heal and repeal his aching, broken traumas.

In the meantime, the beautiful maidens frolicked happily across the countryside in their own divine feminine power. Some even settled and married other knights who were in divine vibrational alignment as they were. This powerful alchemy of pure beauty and energy spread across to neighbouring villages in the countryside.

The Mermaid Who Took Her Fin Off

She was a Piscean soul in the form of a female human body. Yet her mermaid tail represented her intense emotions that precariously ran as deep as the waters of the Pacific. Her soul had plunged into the unknown abyss of imbalance, confusion, incoherence and intoxication. She was left to swim in the deepness of it all. Splashing and struggling within herself against the strong currents of the bottom of the ocean, she delved even deeper into the abyss of unchartered waters that harshly stung the raw, authentic, softness of her skin and the essence of her soul.

She fought to swim against the strong currents that vehemently pulled her soul deeper and deeper. To her dismay, this fighting only pulled her closer to the depths of the ocean floor where ultimately she would plummet to the death of her soul and all that she had known and loved. Being the true Piscean being of light that she was, swimming in past/present/future directions, she began to surrender to the disillusioned stimulation of it all. As she surrendered to the truth of her emotions, she found herself sturdily and peacefully swimming through the now supportive waters that were ever so gently pushing her towards the surface.

With a greater awareness of herself and the truth of who she really was, she excitedly looked forward to stepping foot onto land again. She peered up towards the brim of the water, while reminiscing in profound gratitude for all that she had experienced. At the same time, she eagerly waited for the rest of her journey to unfold in the most uplifting of ways. In her balance, clarity, and freedom, she released the once tormenting waters of emotions and finally took off her fin.

Conclusion

Thank you for reading the short stories and poetry throughout my book. I hope you realize that underneath the layers of pain and suffering you may have experienced throughout your life or are experiencing today, you are worthy and loved beyond all that is conceivable or measured. Your soul is an infinite ray of cosmic lights just waiting for you to shed and release your past hurts, upsets, traumas, and emotional baggage that could still be holding you back or keeping you stuck in life. I hope my book and the messages you receive will help you see that you too can shine and radiate the true brilliance and essence of who you really are.

By going within and doing your inner-child and inner-soul work, you will learn to accept and acknowledge your past hurts and upsets. This work leaves more space for your mind, body, and soul to let go, heal, forgive yourself and others, learn compassion over resentment, and ultimately transform into the best version of yourself.

There are several energy healing and energy tools that I use for myself and for my clients. They are Emotional Freedom Techniques (EFT), Matrix Re-Imprinting, and Quantum EFT for the soul. They are powerful tools that help us shift and release to heal, grow, shine, and radiate into the beautiful beings that we are.

You are worth the investment to heal, grow, transform, radiate, and shine! You are the *Youniverse* that resides within our beautiful cosmic galaxies. All that you ever need is already within you.

You are magnificent.

You are brilliant.

You are worthy of all there is!

Peace, love, and light, beautiful souls.

Namaste,

Gillian

www.eft-transform.com

About the Author

Gillian Small is a Transformational Life Coach, Reiki master, and yoga instructor. She has a private practice, working with people in the comfort of her home studio and over Skype or Zoom with distant clients. In her practice, she utilizes Emotional Freedom Techniques (EFT), Quantum EFT for the Soul, Matrix Re-Imprinting, and Reiki. She is certified and accredited through NeftTI (The National Emotional Freedom Techniques Training Institute of Canada) and AAMET (The Association for the Advancement of Meridian Energy Techniques). Additionally, she holds a diploma in business marketing.

Gillian lives in Ajax, Ontario, Canada, and is married with identical twin boys. Gillian's passions include writing, yoga, running, and listening to Kryon channelings. She explores interests in energy healing, law of attraction, soul work, past lives, and Akashic records. She enjoys travel, cuddles with her boys, and quality time with her family.

Made in the USA
Lexington, KY
28 February 2019